PALOMA BLANCA

Illustrated by PAULA KRANZ

WHAT IF I FEEL...
ANXIOUS

Dados Internacionais de Catalogação na Publicação (CIP) de acordo com ISBD

B236w Barbieri, Paloma Blanca Alves
          What if I feel... anxious / Paloma Blanca Alves Barbieri ; traduzido por Karina Barbosa dos Santos ; ilustrado por Paula Kranz. – Jandira : W. Books, 2025.
          32 p. ; 24cm x 24cm. – (What if I feel...)

          Tradução de: E se eu sentir... ansiedade
          ISBN: 978-65-5294-222-7

          1. Literatura Infantil. 2. Emoções. 3. Sentimentos. 4. Ansiedade. 5. Psicologia. 6. Saúde. 7. Saúde mental. I. Santos, Karina Barbosa dos. II. Kranz, Paula. III. Título. IV. Série.

                                              CDD 028.5
2025-1833   CDU 82-93

Elaborada por Vagner Rodolfo da Silva - CRB-8/9410

Índice para catálogo sistemático:
1. Literatura infantil 028.5
2. Literatura infantil 82-93

This book was printed in Melon Slices and Metallophile font.

This is a W. Books publication, a division of Grupo Ciranda Cultural.
© 2025 Ciranda Cultural Editora e Distribuidora Ltda.
Publisher: Elisângela da Silva
Text © Paloma Blanca A. Barbieri
Illustrations © Paula Kranz
Translation: Karina Barbosa dos Santos
Proofreading: Adriane Gozzo
Design: Fernando Nunes / Cover: Natalia Renzzo

First published in June 2025
www.cirandacultural.com.br

All rights reserved. No part of this publication may be reproduced, stored in a retrieval system, or transmitted in any form or by any means, electronic, mechanical, photocopying, recording, or otherwise, without written permission of the copyright holder, nor may it be circulated bound or covered in any manner other than that in which it was published, or without such conditions beholden to subsequent purchasers.

"Emotions are the colors of the soul; they are spectacular and incredible. When you don't feel, the world becomes dull and colorless."
William P. Young

I dedicate this book to my gigantic family (especially my mother, Creusa), who has given me and continues to give the most beautiful and diverse emotions!

There are moments when I feel a very different kind of emotion within me.

It's strange, confusing, and usually comes all of sudden.

Besides tightening my chest, this emotion makes me sweat.

It also makes me bite my nails and, sometimes, barely allows me to breathe.

It took me a while to understand what this feeling really was.

I even thought it was a mix of sadness, fear, and longing.

But thanks to my parents' help, I found out it was something called **anxiety!**

Even though everyone knows this emotion, Mom says it's usually hard to recognize.

That's why it's important to pay attention to when it appears and the sensations it causes.

I noticed that **anxiety** tends to show up when my birthday or another important date is still far away.

At those times, Mom tells me to take it one day at a time, because that way, days go by and I feel more joy and ease.

Anxiety also shows up if I check my phone all the time.

To prevent this from happening, Dad suggests different games. That makes me feel happier, calmer, and even more confident.

If I keep any kind of fear or worry inside me, I get anxious right away.

But if I do activities that get my body moving, like dancing or running, the anxiety goes away quickly. **Whew!**

I also feel anxious at other moments:
... when I have to change schools...

... when I have a dentist appointment...

... and when I'm the center of attention.

That's because these situations make me feel terrified. They give me butterflies in my stomach and make me really nervous.

Most of the time, **anxiety** triggers strange things in me...

I get a huge craving for sweets.

I feel restless and full of nervous energy.

And sometimes, I even get unexplained insomnia.

I know **anxiety** can show up from time to time, but I've found a way to deal with it:

I do the activities I love and spend time with the people I care about, because that way, both my mind and my **heart** calm down!

How do you feel today?

Afraid

Loving

Anxious

Angry

Jealous

Missing someone

Take a moment to talk about how you're feeling right now.

Talking About Anxiety

To learn how to deal with anxiety, we first need to understand what causes it. It's important to think about and talk about this feeling so that, little by little, we can let it go. Read the questions below and take a moment to reflect on each one:

- What makes you feel anxious?
- How do you act or react when you feel this way?
- When was the last time you felt anxious?
- How did you cope with this feeling?

Just like anger and sadness, anxiety is a common emotion that can affect both kids and adults. Many things can trigger this feeling, such as the first day of school, changing schools, feeling scared, or worrying that something might happen.

Even though it's normal to feel anxious sometimes, it's important to learn how to manage it. If anxiety becomes too overwhelming, it can prevent you from enjoying important moments in your life.

So, whenever anxiety knocks on your heart's door, try doing something that makes you happy or spending time with people you love. And if you feel comfortable, share your feelings with someone you trust.

Children, Animals, and Feelings

Children are fascinated by pets, and it's no wonder why! Besides being loving and great friends, pets bring joy to a home, improve our health, and create a wonderful sense of well-being.

Having a pet (whether it's a kitten, a puppy, or a bunny) can teach children important values like patience, respect, kindness, affection, and responsibility.

Also, when they're with animals, children find the confidence and self-esteem they need to solve their problems and even deal with their own feelings.

A Message for the Family

Discovering emotions can be both exciting and challenging for children, especially when those feelings are difficult to understand. That's why this book aims to help little ones recognize when and how anxiety appears and understand the importance of experiencing it at different moments of life.

During this journey of emotional discovery, families and educators are invited to see anxiety from a different perspective: the child's! After all, children have a unique and special way of looking at the world around them.

Managing emotions isn't always easy, whether for adults or children. That's why the earlier kids learn to understand their feelings, the sooner they'll develop the confidence and independence they need to navigate this incredible journey we all share: life!

PALOMA BLANCA was born in a coastal city in São Paulo. Passionate about languages, she pursued a degree in literature and specialized in translation and teaching.

She has loved writing since childhood; in her stories and poems, she would express everything she felt, as writing became the perfect way for her to explore and understand her emotions. Writing this book has been a true gift, one she hopes to share with families, especially with children who, just like she did in her childhood, wish to learn how to navigate the whirlwind of emotions that arise throughout life.

PAULA KRANZ is the mother of two wonderful girls. When she became a mother, her heart was flooded with countless emotions. She embraced the opportunity to transform all the fear, sadness, anger, and immense joy she experienced into feelings that helped her grow as a person.

Together with her daughters, she reconnected with the magical world of childhood. In recent years, alongside playing pretend, building sandcastles, and doodling, she has also specialized in children's books, illustrating many published works. She is filled with dreams and an eagerness to capture the delicacy and lightness of childhood, bringing to life the magic, the sparkle in children's eyes, and their unique way of seeing the world – something they share with us every single day.